NATTER INTERCEPTOR PROJECT

Reported by
Dr. C.B. MILLIKAN
NavTecMisEu

July 1945

CIOS Target Number 5/182a
Jet Propulsion

COMBINED INTELLIGENCE OBJECTIVES SUB-COMMITTEE
G-2 Division, SHAEF (Rear) APO 413

The Naval & Military Press Ltd

Published by

The Naval & Military Press Ltd
Unit 5 Riverside, Brambleside
Bellbrook Industrial Estate
Uckfield, East Sussex
TN22 1QQ England

Tel: +44 (0)1825 749494

www.naval-military-press.com
www.nmarchive.com

In reprinting in facsimile from the original, any imperfections are inevitably reproduced and the quality may fall short of modern type and cartographic standards.

TABLE OF CONTENTS

	Page
1. Introduction	3
2. History of Project and Intended Tactical Use	3
3. Personnel Interrogated and Their Disposition	4
4. Characteristics of the Airplane and Launcher	5
5. Method of Operation	9
6. Tests	9
7. Present Status	12
8. Recommendations	13

SUMMARY

This report presents the results of an investigation of the Natter Interceptor Project by a naval team consisting of Lt.C.L. Poor, III, USNR, Dr. C.B. Millikan, and Lt. A.Hyatt, USMCR. The bulk of the information was obtained from engineering personnel now located at St.Leonhard, in the Inn Valley, west of Innsbruck.

NATTER INTERCEPTOR PROJECT

1. Introduction.

Prior to the investigation of this target a number of assessment reports were made available to the team, but there was no indication that a complete investigation had been made. The assessments differed widely in their estimates of the importance of the development. It was accordingly decided to make as careful an investigation as possible.

2. History of Project and its Intended Tactical Use.

(a) The project was initiated August 1, 1944, by the Bachem-Werke, Waldsee under the sponsorship of Oberst Knemayer, Chief of Development, RLM. Its purpose was to act as an interceptor against the Allied high altitude bombers. At the end of the war 150 planes were on order by the SS and 50 by the Luftwaffe. The designers were Herr Bachem, formerly Technical Director of Fieseler, and Herr Bothbeder, a Dutchman who had studied at Stuttgart, was brought to Germany in 1940, and worked at Dornier before joining Bachem. Late in April the factory was dispersed, Bachem remaining in Waldsee, and Bothbeder with a group of technicians taking four (4) planes to St. Leonhard, where they were when the U. S. Army arrived. Before the dispersal Bachem had some 600 workers of whom about 300 were engaged on Natter, including approximately 60 engineers. It was planned that production on a considerable scale would be carried out in a large number of small factories and shops scattered over Germany. The design had been very consistently worked out so that only unskilled workers and the most common and readily available materials would be required. Lightness and complexity were everywhere sacrificed in the interest of economy, simplicity, and absence of elaborate jigging and construction tools. The plane was to be used as a "one-shot" device being destroyed after its initial flight and contact with the enemy. The basic materials used were the commonest grades of wood and the cheapest quality steel.

(b) The German government had planned to sell the Natter plans and all construction details to the Japanese. The engineers interrogated were unable to tell whether or not this plan had been executed, and it is believed that they were actually ignorant in this connection. The plane should be tactically very useful to the Japs

2. History of Project and its Intended Tactical Use (b) (Cont'd.)

and the type of construction should be highly suited to manufacture in Japan. The possibility that Japan may be able to undertake the project is, accordingly, one of its most significant features.

3. Personnel Interrogated and Their Disposition.

(a) The following members of the Natter group had been held for some weeks at Camp Haiming. After careful interrogation of the key persons, the entire group was returned to the town of Jerzens near Wenns. This was approved by the Military Government officer at the camp. All of the men were instructed to report daily to the Burgomeister of Jerzens and to be available for further interrogation should this be desired. The house number where each man lives is indicated opposite his name:

H. Bethbeder	20	R. Granzow	32
G. Schaller	30	K. Schaller	30
H. Zuebert	142	H. Jonas	142

(b) Bethbeder, who speaks and understands English fairly well, was interrogated for several hours and furnished most of the information on the project. He was very cooperative and apparently withheld no information on matters of interest. He impressed the team as an extremely ingenious and capable engineer. The project has so many unorthodox and unusual features that it is apt to appear unrealistic and "crackpot". Bethbeder was able, however, to demonstrate that each of the unorthodox elements had been carefully worked out and engineered in accordance with a consistent and very reasonable conception of the overall problem.

(c) Zuebert was the test pilot for the project and furnished considerable information on the flying characteristics of the glider version which he had flown.

(d) Granzow was Walter's representative on the project and was responsible for the functioning of the main rocket motor. He contributed relatively little to the team's knowledge.

(e) G. Schaller was sent by RLM as a liaison man and inspector for development and production. It was stated that he might have been a Nazi party member, but that he had not been active in the

3. Personnel Interrogated and Their Disposition (e) (Cont'd.)

party. His interrogation contributed little.

(f) K. Schaller and Jonas were talked to only very briefly, since they apparently were workers who knew very little about the project.

(g) Bachem, who was co-designer with Bethbeder, remained at Waldsee when Bethbeder's group evacuated to the Inn Valley. He planned to bury a complete set of Natter drawings and technical data in the Waldsee area. It was agreed that he and Bethbeder would later attempt to establish contact by leaving messages at the latter's ski hut "Einen Eckalpe" at Oberstaufen, 15 kilometers from Isny. This town is near Kempten south of Augsburg. The rendezvous has not yet been effected but Bethbeder believes that Bachem is probably in the neighborhood of Isny, and is confident that he, Bethbeder, could find him.

4. Characteristics of the Airplane and Launcher.

(a) The Natter is essentially a very inexpensive single seat, rocket powered interceptor, which is launched vertically from a short launcher, controlled by an auto-pilot to a position predetermined by a standard anti-aircraft flak computer as being in the neighborhood of an enemy bomber, and guided by the pilot to the target at very high speed. At a distance of a few hundred yards twenty-four (24) - 73 millimeter rockets are fired in a burst and Natter dives away. When clear of the enemy the speed is reduced to 200-300 km./hr., the nose and then the remainder of the plane are jettisoned, and the pilot parachutes to the ground.

(b) The basic numerical data (as furnished from memory by Bethbeder) are as follows:

```
Designation - - - - - - - - - Bachem 8-349 A 1 "Natter".
Initial weight with 4 boost rockets - - - - 2200 kg.
Gross weight including fuel but
   without boost rockets - - - - - - - - - - 1700 kg.
Fuel weight - - - - - - - - - - - - - - - - -  650 kg.
Wing area - - - - - - - - - - - - - - - - - -  3.6 m².
Wing span - - - - - - - - - - - - - - - - - -  3.6 m.
Horiz. tail area - - - - - - - - - - - - - -   2.5 m².
Horiz. tail span - - - - - - - - - - - - - -   2.5 m.
```

4. Characteristics of the Airplane and Launcher (b) (Cont'd.)

Wing and horizontal tail: Rectangular plan form, no dihedral, no sweepback, constant profile 12 percent thickness at 50 percent chord, symmetrical section. Tail setting—1° to wing. Vertical surface approximately 2/3 above fuselage and 1/3 below. No ailerons, roll control by differential operation of elevators. Overall length——6 m.

C_{D_p} (at M=0.4) = 0.08 from wind tunnel tests.

Launcher is circular tube projecting vertically 9 m. from the ground.

Boost: 4 Schmidding rockets (SG 34) each having 12,000 kg. sec. impulse with a nominal burning time of 10 sec.

Main Power Plant: Walter 509 A-2 rocket motor burning C and T stoffs. Max. thrust = 1700 kg.

Regulation possible down to 150 kg.

Fuel consumption = 5.5 gm. per kg. sec. at sea level full thrust.

= 10 gm. per kg. sec. at sea level at 300 kg. thrust.

Armament: 24 - 73 mm. rockets each weighing 2.6 kg. and containing 400 gm. of powder in the warhead. For later versions 48 rockets were planned.

Design max. level speed = 800 km./hr. at s.l.

Range (radius of action) after reaching 12 km. height ≅ 40 km.

Stressed for 6 g. acceleration at 1100 km./hr. at 3 km. altitude with a factor of safety of 1.5 based on ultimate strength.

Materials: Low grade wood and steel throughout except for motor, fuel tanks and piping, and main wing spar.

4. Characteristics of the Airplane and Launchers(b) (Cont'd.)

Construction: Extremely simple and crude. Wood parts universally joined with glue and nails. Fittings heavy and simple. The entire design has been systematically and carefully worked out for rapid and cheap construction by inexperienced workers in small, poorly-equipped shops. Weight and refinement of finish were consciously sacrificed for this purpose. Bethbeder gave the following figures for man-hours required to construct the machine in small scale production:

Airframe	250 man-hours
Motor	400 man-hours
Rockets, Instruments, etc.	350 man-hours
Total aircraft	1000 man-hours

4. Characteristics of the Airplane and Launcher (b) (Cont'd.)

The sketches indicate very roughly the general arrangement.

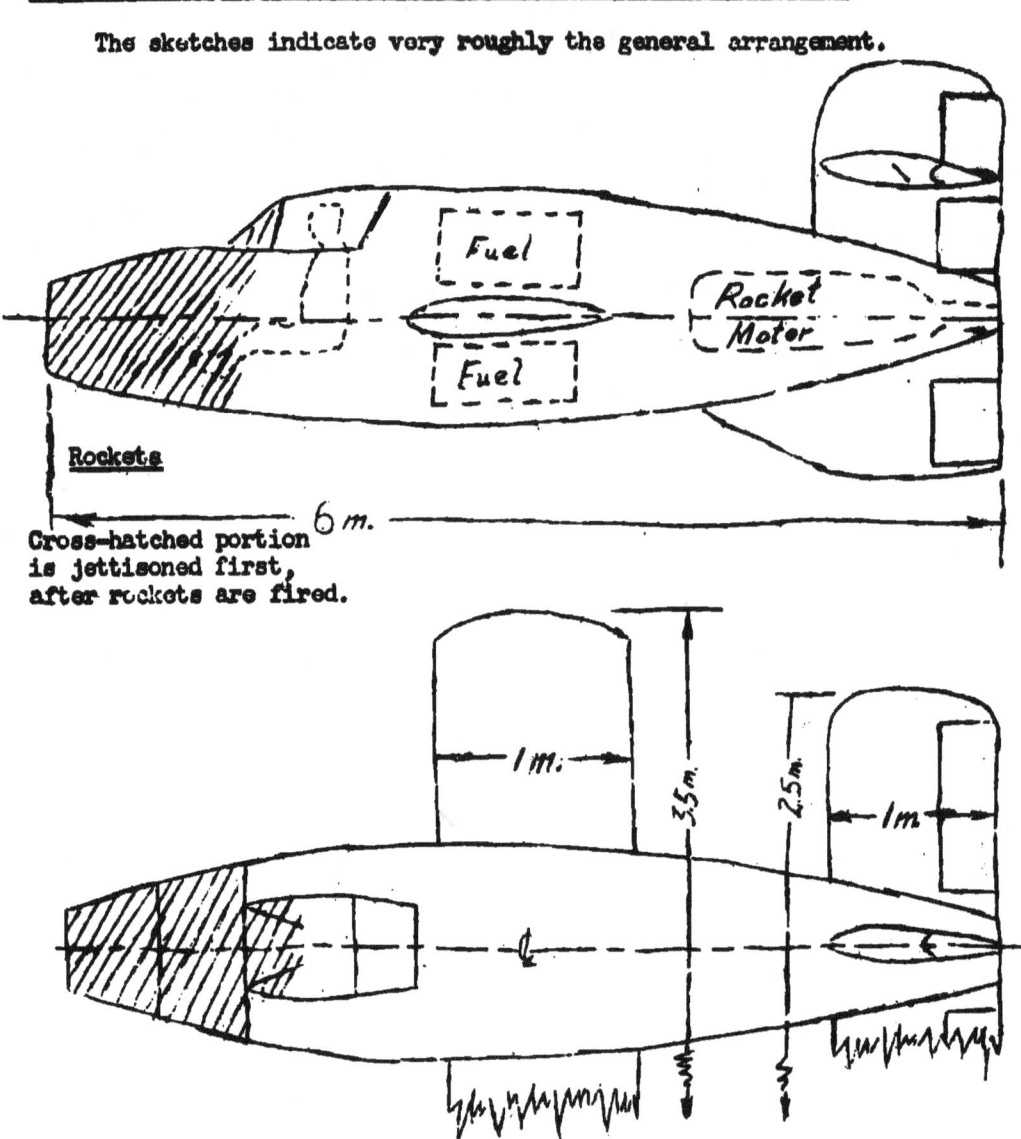

Rockets

Cross-hatched portion is jettisoned first, after rockets are fired.

5. Method of Operation.

The plane is attached to the launching tube on which it can slide vertically and around which it can rotate. A standard anti-aircraft director is placed alongside and the orientation of the plane is set, as is the elevator deflection required at the end of the vertically flight so that a straight flight path will reach the predicted location of the enemy bomber. The motor and launching rockets are fired and the plane ascends vertically some 150 meters when the auto-pilot deflects the elevators and holds the plane on the predetermined straight, climbing flight path. At this time the boost rockets are dropped. When the pilot sights the enemy he takes over and when on the target and in range fires the 24 rockets. He then dives away and when clear slows to about 250 km./hr. and releases the nose section which is sucked forward and clear by the pressure distribution over it. The pilot then releases a parachute from the rear of the fuselage. The latter decelerates very rapidly ejecting the pilot who parachutes to the ground.

6. Tests. (As reported by Bethbeder and Zuebert)

Wind tunnel tests on models were made in September 1944 at DVL at 500 km./hr., and in the high speed tunnel at Braunschweig in March 1945 at speeds close to $M=1$. No bad effects of compressibility on stability or control were reported.

Approximately a dozen launching and glide tests were made on the first 15 planes produced. This flight test program appears to have been unusually thoroughly and carefully done, in view of the pressure from the government for service models. The auto-pilot development was delayed to the extent that only one flight was attempted with this control installed. The most important results of these tests are summarized below:

(a) **Vertical Launching, Unmanned.**

The most radical feature of the project, from an aerodynamic viewpoint, is the vertical launching from a short launcher. In spite of the initial acceleration of some 2 g., the velocity at the time of leaving the launcher is far too low (some 50 to 60 km./hr.) for the aerodynamic forces on wing and tail to have any stabilizing effect. The problem is aggravated by the extreme

6. Tests (a) (Cont'd.)

rearward c.g. position at 0.60 chord when the four loaded boost rockets are installed at the rear of the fuselage. The c.g. after jettisoning the boost rockets lies between 18 percent and 25 percent chord depending on the amount of fuel and armament present. In order to obtain stability with the rear c.g. position; auxiliary surfaces 1 meter square were attached to each stabilizer tip with explosive bolts. This modification increased the tail span during the launching period to 4.5 m. The explosive bolts were fired, dropping the auxiliary tail tips, when the boost rockets were jettisoned.

In a number of the unmanned tests the boost rockets exploded, destroying the airplane. In general the Schmidding boost rockets were felt to be unsatisfactory, both because of the occasional explosions and also because the duration of burning and hence the thrust varied by as much as 100 percent from rocket to rocket.

Part of the launchings were made with 25 percent c.g. position without tail tips and part with 60 percent c.g. position with tail tips. In all cases where the boost rockets did not explode the plane rose vertically to a height of approximately 150 meters without any unsteadiness or oscillation. At this altitude the speed was sufficient for the aerodynamic surfaces to become effective and the plane continued its flight as a conventionally stabilized and controlled airplane. Bethbeder explained the remarkable stability of the initial slow speed flight by suggesting that the jet itself exerted a stabilizing influence.

In the majority of these flights, small aileron-type tabs were mounted on the wing so that the plane executed slow rolls during the climb above some 200 m. altitude. A maximum altitude of some 3 km. was reached on these uncontrolled flights.

One test was made with a 3-element auto-pilot control, but the 3 elements had not been properly synchronized and the flight was very erratic. Further tests with auto-pilot were abandoned pending the completion of development on this device.

Bethbeder was not satisfied with the droppable tail tips, and accordingly designed and tested thin metal jet control vanes, to give control during launching. These vanes would eliminate the necessity for the tail tips. They were cooled by a small supply

6. Tests (a) (Cont'd.)

of water which boiled away in about 30 seconds after which the vanes burned up and disappeared. This device would have been used on later tests.

(b) <u>Glide Tests</u>.

One manned glide test was made in which there was no motor and the plane was ballasted to a gross weight of 1700 kg. with c.g. at 25 percent chord. The plane was towed to an altitude of 5500 m. by a He 111 and then released. The following flight characteristics were noted by the pilot:

(1) Stability was excellent and controls light and well coordinated for indicated air speeds between 200 and 700 km./hr.

(2) There was no rolling moment due to sideslip, and no apparent yawing moment due to differential deflection of the elevators to produce roll. These characteristics had been designed into the plane.

(3) The rate of roll was estimated at 1 rev. per sec.

(4) At 400 km./hr. a full circle could be turned in approximately 20 secs.

(5) The controlled stalling speed was 200 km./hr. indicated air speed which occurred at an angle of attack of about $30°$.

(6) The handling and flying qualities were judged by the pilot to be superior to those of any of the standard German single-seat fighters.

On this flight the explosive bolts which released the nose section failed to operate and the pilot released the cockpit enclosure and bailed out in the normal manner. In two unmanned glide tests the nose jettisoning mechanism did; however, function correctly. On later models a mechanical release replaced the explosive bolts.

The final sequence of operations for the jettisoning procedure is as follows:

6. Tests (b) (Cont'd.)

(1) The pilot releases his harness which permits him to lean forward so as to uncouple the stick from the control system and swing it forward into a horizontal position where it latches and releases the safety on the nose release attachments.

(2) The pilot then releases the mechanical connections holding the nose section, which is immediately pulled off and far forward of the fuselage due to the high suction over its forward portion. The nose carries with it the instrument panel, windshield, firewall armor plate, and rudder pedals, leaving the space ahead of the pilot completely open.

(3) A small, extremely strong parachute is then released from a well near the rear of the fuselage. It is attached to the fuselage by two steel cables each nearly ½ inch in diameter. When the parachute opens the fuselage is violently decelerated, ejecting the pilot forward out of his seat and clear of the plane.

(4) The pilot opens his chute and descends to the ground.

(c) **Manned Launching**.

A single manned launching was attempted. On this flight the vertical start was normal. At a height of some 150 m. the cockpit cover (carrying the headrest) flew off and the plane turned on its back as if the stick had been pulled back. It climbed inverted at some 15° to the horizontal until it reached a height of some 1500 meters then dived on its back to the ground, killing the pilot.

There are a number of possible explanations of the accident, the most probable being that the cockpit cover latch was not secured and that the pilot was knocked out when the cockpit cover and headrest flew off. Further manned tests were scheduled but could not be carried out before the evacuation caused by the allied advance.

7. Present Status.

(a) Bachem is supposed to have buried the complete plans and specifications in the Waldsee area. He presumably is also cognizant as to the extent to which the Japanese dealings had progressed. Bethbeder believes that he could locate Bachem and obtain the

7. Present Status.(a) (Cont'd.)

documents and information.

(b) An incomplete set of drawings which Bothbeder had had with him were turned over to a group 4 Caft team, CIOS. These documents were sent from the specialist camp, G-2 Hdqtrs., 6th A.G. through normal CIOS channels and will presumably be available for further study

(c) A CIOS report by Capt. Bratt, AAF and F/Lt. Evans dated approximately 30 May has been sent to USSTAF and through channels. The existence of this investigation and report was unknown to the present team until after their investigation was completed. The numerical data of the CIOS and present reports are in good agreement.

(d) Two fairly complete planes found at St. Leonhard were evacuated and turned over to the Disarmament Group, Munich. Presumably they will be shipped to Wright Field and the U. K.

(e) Capt. Bratt reports that 3 or 4 planes are at Wolf Hirth Flugzeugbau at Naborn unter Teck (S2704). These planes are 50 percent to 75 percent completed and could fairly readily be finished if more units are desired.

(f) Letter Report 28-45 (to CNO from NavTecMisEu, 21 May 1945) was consulted during the preparation of the present report. The numerical values given in the Letter Report are, in some cases, quite different from those given here and in the CIOS report mentioned above. It is believed that the present data are the more accurate.

8. Recommendations.

(a) The successful, vertical launching technique and the water-cooled jet vanes are of considerable technical interest. The pertinent information should be made available to persons concerned with interceptor aircraft, guided missiles, and rocket motors.

(b) The flying characteristics and unusual armament warrant further study by airplane designers and "military requirements" personnel.

-13-

8. Recommendations (Cont'd.)

(c) The amount of Natter material turned over to Japan should be ascertained if possible. The use of Bethbeder to find Bachem for interrogation should be considered in this connection.

(d) If it appears that Japan may be actively working on Natter, the difficult problem of counter-measures should be undertaken promptly.

(e) Since Natter is essentially a defensive weapon, it is not likely that it should be directly useful to the U. S. in military or naval campaigns which are likely to occur in the near future. Certain of the special features of Natter might, however, be usefully applied in the development of offensive weapons.

Prepared by:

C. B. MILLIKAN,
Technician.

www.ingramcontent.com/pod-product-compliance
Lightning Source LLC
Chambersburg PA
CBHW081509040426
42446CB00017B/3449